Dear Yelina

In His Marvelous Love
Bet Amante

Terra Cotta

A collection of inspirational poems and Scriptures penned as the product of one believer's personal experience with the Lord Jesus Christ

Bet Howard Amante

WESTBOW
PRESS
A DIVISION OF THOMAS NELSON
& ZONDERVAN

Copyright © 2015 Bet Howard Amante.

All rights reserved. No part of this book may be used or reproduced by any means, graphic, electronic, or mechanical, including photocopying, recording, taping or by any information storage retrieval system without the written permission of the publisher except in the case of brief quotations embodied in critical articles and reviews.

This book is a work of non-fiction. Unless otherwise noted, the author and the publisher make no explicit guarantees as to the accuracy of the information contained in this book and in some cases, names of people and places have been altered to protect their privacy.

Scripture taken from the King James Version of the Bible.

WestBow Press books may be ordered through booksellers or by contacting:

WestBow Press
A Division of Thomas Nelson & Zondervan
1663 Liberty Drive
Bloomington, IN 47403
www.westbowpress.com
1 (866) 928-1240

Because of the dynamic nature of the Internet, any web addresses or links contained in this book may have changed since publication and may no longer be valid. The views expressed in this work are solely those of the author and do not necessarily reflect the views of the publisher, and the publisher hereby disclaims any responsibility for them.

Any people depicted in stock imagery provided by Thinkstock are models, and such images are being used for illustrative purposes only. Certain stock imagery © Thinkstock.

ISBN: 978-1-4908-8392-2 (sc)
ISBN: 978-1-4908-8393-9 (hc)
ISBN: 978-1-4908-8391-5 (e)

Library of Congress Control Number: 2015909791

Print information available on the last page.

WestBow Press rev. date: 06/30/2015

2 Corinthians 4:6–7

For God, who commanded the light to shine out of darkness, hath shined in our hearts, to give the light of the knowledge of the glory of God in the face of Jesus Christ. But we have this treasure in earthen vessels, that the excellency of the power may be of God, and not of us.

Dedicated to the man who loves me and believes in my work,
my husband,
my encourager, and my best friend,
Gene D. Amante.

Contents

A Mother's Dreams 1
At His Feet 4
Broken 6
Compassion 8
Discontentment 10
Embers 13
Feelings 15
First Light 17
Heaven's Rose 19
Is It Easy 21
Justice 24
Leaving 26
Limelight 28
Light Sensitive 31
My Cross 33
My Mark 36
My Preference 38
No Applause 41
One Small Boy 44
On Paper 47
Resurrection Power 49
Sharing Life 52
Sunday Morning Sunrise 54
The Day 56
The Holy One 58
The Lost Sheep 61
The Lamb's Prayer 63
The Mystery 65
The Nativity 67
The Real Jesus 71

The Two-Edged Sword 73
The Watchman 76
Traveling Clothes 81
What Has Been Done 83
What Works.. 86
Wilderness 88
Will You Gamble 91
Words 95
Wounded Pride 97

Introduction

At the tender young age of five years, I heard the Lord speak to me very clearly. His message was simple, one a child could understand. I was running barefoot through our neighbor's yard one sunny summer day when I heard Him say, "Look up." I stopped in my tracks and looked up to see who had spoken to me. Then I heard the voice again, saying, "I am God. You will remember this day and this moment throughout your lifetime. You will never forget." I have never forgotten. I can even remember the pink, ruffled sun-suit I was wearing.

I heard that same voice during a church service when I was ten. I recognized it instantly, and I understood the message: "I have called you unto Myself and will send you forth into this world to share My Word." I had just completed vacation Bible school Sunday in our little, white Methodist church in Matagorda, Texas, and was delighted to receive and publicly proclaim Jesus as my Savior. I was baptized the following Sunday, April 9, 1950, and was called by the Lord to minister the gospel. How could I forget? I thought surely the Lord would send me to either Africa or China. Where else would He send me?

When I announced my religious calling to friends and family, they smiled. Some laughed. Some said, "Well, how sweet," or, "You have got to be kidding." No one took me seriously … but God.

It was thirty-one years later, on April 9, 1970, that I heard the Lord speak to me again. While alone, without hope, and suicidal, I dropped to my knees in front of my kitchen sink. I heard the Lord say, "It's time to come home." I totally surrendered my life to the Lord.

That was forty-four years ago. It was the best decision I ever made. My life was instantly changed by the grace of God. I became a new creation. Old things passed away, and all things became new.

I still obey His voice. Every day is full of hope and the promise of eternal life, with joy unspeakable and full of glory. God is faithful to perform that which He has purposed for the life of every believer. I am living proof of His goodness and mercy.

> Bless the Lord, O my soul: and all that is within me, bless his holy name. Bless the Lord, O my soul, and forget not all his benefits: Who forgiveth all thine iniquities; who healeth all thy diseases; Who redeemeth thy life from destruction; who crowneth thee with lovingkindness and tender mercies; Who satisfieth thy mouth with good things; so that thy youth is renewed like the eagle's. (Psalm 103:1–5)

This collection of poems was written to minister faith and God's love to all who need inspiration and assurance in the God who loves us completely.

> Being confident of this very thing, that he which hath begun a good work in you will perform *it* until the day of Jesus Christ. (Philippians 1:5–6)

A Mother's Dreams

Our children all so need to hear
Words of praise caress their ears.
Young or old, they're still the same;
They love the mention of their names.

Just to know that there is space
Within each heart, a special place
For loving thoughts and sweet desires,
Fond memories of glowing fires.

And childhood dreams left unfulfilled
Still hold fast in hope strong-willed.
Joys and sorrows, so much love,
Life's bittersweet velvet glove.

Touch now my mind with gentle trace
And silhouette each darling face
Like shadows, lingering through the day,
Toward the evening fade away.

How suddenly I have grown old.
No chubby little hands to hold.
My three sons are now grown men.
I see them only now and then.

Regrets, oh yes, how could I not.
I made mistakes, perhaps a lot.
And yet there lies within my breast
A joyful sense of peace and rest.

For I have loved each child, without
The slightest trace of any doubt.
And the greatest thing this mom could do
Was introduce them, Lord, to You.

> Train up a child in the way he should go: and when he is old, he will not depart from it. (Proverbs 22:6)

> And all thy children shall be taught of the Lord; and great shall be the peace of thy children. In righteousness shalt thou be established: thou shalt be far from oppression; for thou shalt not fear: and from terror; for it shall not come near thee. Behold, they shall surely gather together, but not by me: whosoever shall gather together against thee shall fall for thy sake. Behold, I have created the smith that bloweth the coals in the fire, and that bringeth forth an instrument for his work; and I have created the waster to destroy. No weapon that is formed

against thee shall prosper; and every tongue that shall rise against thee in judgment thou shalt condemn. This is the heritage of the servants of the Lord, and their righteousness is of me, saith the Lord. (Isaiah 54:13–17)

At His Feet

As I sit at the feet of my Lord,
With the dawning of each new day,
He tenderly places His nail-scarred hand
On my shoulder and waits as I pray.

"I have stumbled and fallen, dear Master.
I'm not worthy to mention Your name.
And the cross is so heavy to carry,"
Are the words I confess in my shame.

"My child, I have walked before you,
And I know the temptations you face.
Time and again you will stumble and fall,
As did I when I carried the cross in your place.

"Hold fast, and remember, when under the load
As the strength of my body gave way,
God the Father provided another to carry
The cross up the hill on that day.

"Lift up your head, and look into my eyes,"
Jesus whispers, and His words are so sweet.
"You're forgiven, My child. Now rest in Me,
For in Me you're already complete.

"There is no condemnation
For those who believe in My name.
Because I love you, I paid the price.
You are Mine; I have taken your blame."

Now I sit at the feet of my Lord,
With the dawning of each new day.
And the joy of His presence surrounds me
As He hears every word that I say.

How I praise Thee, dear Jesus, my Master.
How I love Thee with all my heart.
And in humbleness, Lord, I'm so thankful
That from me You will never depart.

> There is therefore now no condemnation to them which are in Christ Jesus who walk not after the flesh, but after the Spirit. (Romans 8:1)
>
> Teaching them to observe all that I have commanded you. And behold I am with you always, to the end of the age. (Matthew 28:20)
>
> So we can confidently say, "The Lord is my helper I will not fear what can man do to me?" (Hebrews 13:6)
>
> Do not be anxious about anything, but in everything by prayer and supplication with thanksgiving let your requests be made known to God. And the peace of God, which surpasses all understanding, will guard your hearts and your minds in Christ Jesus. (Philippians 4:6–7)

Broken

No, not again, Lord, I cannot allow the breaking.
Not one more time, or this heart will never mend.
Is there no way to relieve the endless aching?
How much longer can I manage to pretend?

Until lately, I've been successful at stonewalling,
But the pressure is increasing day by day.
How much longer can I keep the tears from falling?
I would crumble if the floodgates should give way.

And how can I fit the pieces back together?
I no longer have the wherewithal to try.
'Tis not a question of my will, but whether
I can find within my heart a reason why.

No, not again, Lord. I cannot go through the anguish.
Please don't tell me I must ever trust again.
At the thought of vulnerability I languish,
For I've known trusting as the precursor to pain.

Yet You tell me that the opposite of trusting
Is the way that always leads to unbelief.
Once the heart is set in stone, there's no adjusting,
And there is no guarantee of pain relief.

I don't understand, but Lord, it really doesn't matter.
All I know is that You're everything to me.
And if all my hopes and dreams of this world shatter,
I have hope in You throughout eternity.

And the life that You have given me, I'll treasure.
Oh precious Lamb of God, for sinners slain,
You have given love to me beyond all measure.
Here's my heart, dear Lord, be pleased to rule and reign.

> Yea, though I walk through the valley of the shadow of death, I will fear no evil: for thou [art] with me; thy rod and thy staff they comfort me. (Psalm 23:4)
>
> Trust in the Lord with all thine heart; and lean not unto thine own understanding. (Proverbs 3:5–6)
>
> These things I have spoken unto you, that in me ye might have peace. In the world ye shall have tribulation: but be of good cheer; I have overcome the world. (John 16:33)
>
> And not only [so], but we glory in tribulations also: knowing that tribulation worketh patience. (Romans 5:3)
>
> For I reckon that the sufferings of this present time [are] not worthy [to be compared] with the glory which shall be revealed in us. (Romans 8:18)

Compassion

Oh compassion, lift again thy lovely head
To survey the wounded through the Master's eyes.
Let thy healing wings of mercy gently spread
O'er the fallen one whose soul in silence cries.

'Tis the balm of Gilead that must be poured,
The oil of gladness from the Spirit flow
Through the saints on earth, the body of the Lord,
Whose head is Christ; God has ordained it so.

As His body that was broken for our sake,
So are we to be in turn for every soul
Whose infirmities have caused God's heart to break.
Yet through the breaking we have been made whole.

Are we, now that we've been rescued by God's grace,
To despise the flaws we see within all flesh?
If indeed we do, it is to our disgrace,
And we break the loving heart of God afresh.

Let not the swell of arrogance and pride
Replace the contrite honesty within.
Let all haughtiness of self be set aside
To be filled with God's compassion for all men.

> And be ye kind one to another, tenderhearted, forgiving one another, even as God for Christ's sake hath forgiven you. (Ephesians 4:32)

Put on therefore, as the elect of God, holy and beloved, bowels of mercies, kindness, humbleness of mind, meekness, longsuffering; (Colossians 3:12)

Bear ye one another's burdens, and so fulfil the law of Christ. (Galatians 6:2)

Therefore all things whatsoever ye would that men should do to you, do ye even so to them: for this is the law and the prophets. (Matthew 7:12)

Discontentment

Heavenly Father, remind me,
When e'er I start to stray
From the straight and narrow path
To seek a more comfortable way,

When I start to murmur,
Discontented with my lot,
To complain about my portion
And the things I haven't got,

Help me to remember,
When I'm tempted to despair
Because the world around me
Seems so cruel and unfair,

Remind me who I am, Lord,
Of where I am, and why.
Remind me of the reason
That You came to earth to die.

Not for temporary gain,
Nor to save my human pride;
It was not to satisfy my flesh
That You were crucified,

But for that which is eternal:
To provide for me a place
Where I may live forever
In the bounty of Your grace.

And if I look for sources
Within this earthly plain
To satisfy my longing,
My search will end in vain.

Discontentment is a symptom
That reveals my heart's intent
To fulfill my carnal cravings
And my need to repent.

> And he said unto them, Take heed, and beware of covetousness: for a man's life consisteth not in the abundance of the things which he possesseth. (Luke 12:15)

> Delight thyself also in the LORD; and he shall give thee the desires of thine heart. (Psalms 37:4)

But godliness with contentment is great gain. (1 Timothy 6:6–10)

In every thing give thanks: for this is the will of God in Christ Jesus concerning you. (1 Thessalonians 5:18)

Embers

Holy Spirit, stir the embers
That within my heart reside.
Set ablaze the lifeless members
Of Your temple sanctified.

As I reach beyond the portals,
Past the borders of my mind,
To behold that which mere mortals
In the flesh shall never find,

There beneath the visions shattered,
Buried long within the sod,
Burning coals in ashes scattered,
Kindled by the breath of God.

Cloven tongues of confirmation
On my head need never show,
But the joy of my salvation
In my heart remains aglow.

'Tis the all-consuming fire
Rising up within my breast
That fulfills my heart's desire,
God's own presence manifest.

> "John answered, saying unto them all, I indeed baptize you with water; but one mightier than I cometh, the latchet of whose shoes I am not worthy to unloose: he shall baptize you with the Holy Ghost and with fire." (Luke 3:16)

Thou wilt shew me the path of life: in thy presence [is] fulness of joy; at thy right hand [there are] pleasures for evermore. (Psalms 16:11)

And he said, My presence shall go [with thee], and I will give thee rest. (Exodus 33:14)

[When thou saidst], Seek ye my face; my heart said unto thee, Thy face, LORD, will I seek. (Psalms 27:8)

Blessed [are] the pure in heart: for they shall see God. (Matthew 5:8)

Rest in the LORD, and wait patiently for him: fret not thyself because of him who prospereth in his way, because of the man who bringeth wicked devices to pass. (Psalms 37:7–9)

Behold, I stand at the door, and knock: if any man hear my voice, and open the door, I will come in to him, and will sup with him, and he with me. (Revelation 3:20)

But the Comforter, [which is] the Holy Ghost, whom the Father will send in my name, he shall teach you all things, and bring all things to your remembrance, whatsoever I have said unto you. (John 14:26)

And ye shall seek me, and find [me], when ye shall search for me with all thy heart. (Jeremiah 29:13)

Feelings

Feelings are like wisps of smoke
That suddenly appear;
Intimidating words provoke
Proclivity to fear.

Thoughts paralyze the victim's mind,
Imagination's guise;
Fear makes a prey of all mankind
Who listen to its lies.

'Tis but a picture painted by
The enemy, who feeds
Upon emotions tainted by
Deception's deadly seeds.

And all who entertain his thoughts
And find the thoughts appealing,
Shall by indulging self be caught;
Do not give in to feelings.

> [This] I say then, Walk in the Spirit, and ye shall not fulfil the lust of the flesh. (Galatians 5:16)
>
> Wherefore, my beloved brethren, let every man be swift to hear, slow to speak, slow to wrath. (James 1:19)
>
> Looking diligently lest any man fail of the grace of God; lest any root of bitterness springing up trouble [you], and thereby many be defiled. (Hebrews 12:15)

[Let your] conversation [be] without covetousness; [and be] content with such things as ye have: for he hath said, I will never leave thee, nor forsake thee. (Hebrews 13:5)

Then came Peter to him, and said, Lord, how oft shall my brother sin against me, and I forgive him? Jesus saith unto him, I say not unto thee, Until seven times: but, Until seventy times seven. (Matthew 18:21–22)

But he giveth more grace. Wherefore he saith, God resisteth the proud, but giveth grace unto the humble. (James 4:6)

And whatsoever ye do in word or deed, [do] all in the name of the Lord Jesus, giving thanks to God and the Father by him. (Colossians 3:17)

First Light

Beautiful is the golden dawn,
As I rise from spiritual slumber
To behold the sun as it pours forth light,
Transforming shadows of purple and umber.

'Til at last the earth in splendor
Is revealed in sparkling dew.
All creation seems to echo the words,
"Behold, I make all things new."

Softly each gentle ray of light
Caresses the still strings of morn,
Crescendoing while the sweet song of birds
Bursts forth, and a symphony is born.

Life stirs, colored leaves begin to dance;
They twirl in the autumn breeze.
With brilliance they blanket the earth as they fall
Beneath orange and scarlet-topped trees.

Alleluia! My heart joins the chorus.
Alleluia! Rejoicing in praise.
Singing glory to God in the highest!
In worship, His banner is raised.

Thou hast come a light into the world;
Whosoever believeth in Thee
Shall not abide in the darkness still;
Thou hast given us eyes to see.

Thou didst cause mine eyes to open there
In the early morning mist;
All the shadows soon were lifted away
As the sun my eyelids kissed.

Thou hast made my path as a shining light,
Though narrow is the way;
In Thy presence it shineth more and more
Unto the perfect day.

> But the path of the just as the shining light that shineth more and more unto the perfect day. (Proverbs 4:18)
>
> Arise, shine; for thy light is come, and the glory of the LORD is risen upon thee. (Isaiah 60:1)
>
> And blessed [be] his glorious name for ever: and let the whole earth be filled [with] his glory; Amen, and Amen. (Psalms 72:19)
>
> Then a cloud covered the tent of the congregation, and the glory of the LORD filled the tabernacle. (Exodus 40:34–35)
>
> That the God of our Lord Jesus Christ, the Father of glory, may give unto you the spirit of wisdom and revelation in the knowledge of him. (Ephesians 1:17–21)
>
> For the earth shall be filled with the knowledge of the glory of the LORD, as the waters cover the sea. (Habakkuk 2:14)

Heaven's Rose

Oh, let these eyes ne'er fail to see
The glorious one who created me;
The one who reigns upon the throne
Of heaven has made me His own.

With His own blood, my sins erased,
And in my heart His Spirit placed.
The knowledge of His presence there
Brings joy, and heaven fills the air.

Oh, Rose of Sharon, sweetest bloom,
Fill now my life with Your perfume.
And I shall make my heart Your throne
Until these eyes behold Your own.

I am the rose of Sharon, and the lily of the valleys. As the lily among thorns, so is my love among the daughters. As the apple tree among the trees of the wood, so is my beloved among the sons. I sat down under his shadow with great delight, and his fruit was sweet to my taste. (Song of Solomon 2:1–3)

Beloved, now are we the sons of God and it doth not yet appear what we shall be: but we know that, when he shall appear we shall be like him; for we shall see him as he is. (John 3:2)

Is It Easy

Is it easy to consider
The other person's side?
When your feelings have been injured,
How important is your pride?

And if you've been offended
By what someone else has said,
Is it easier to remember
Or forget the past instead?

Is it easy to forgive someone
Whose words have pierced your heart?
When clearly you're the target
Of a painful, fiery dart.

Does your own imagination
And your reasoning run wild?
Is it easy to contain them
Once your temper has been riled?

Is it easy to ignore a fault
Or does it drive you up the wall?
Do you think they had it coming
When you see that person fall?

When you simply can't communicate
And the door slams in your face,
Is it easier to be patient
Or to put them in their place?

Can you justify your anger?
Do you feel you have a right?
Is it easy to resist the urge
To stand your ground and fight?

Is it easy to deny yourself
When faced with strong temptation?
Will you turn the other cheek today
And resist retaliation?

And what about the times when you
Are willfully mistreated?
Can you choose to disregard it
When an offense is repeated?

Is it easy? No, it isn't.
Jesus never said it would be.
But He did say, you must bear the cross
If you choose to follow Me.

And He also said, I'm with you.
And, the things you cannot do,
If you will put your trust in me,
My strength will see you through.

He will turn each tear of sorrow
Into blessings and great joy,
And for you it will be easy
When His power you employ.

Is it easy? Oh, so very
To let go of all your cares,
Once you decide that Jesus
Is in charge of your affairs.

He is Lord, and it's so easy
For the Lord to plead your case.
Not only will He free you,
But your debts He will erase.

There is only one condition,
Each and every day you live;
If you choose to follow Jesus,
You must learn to forgive.

Is it easy? No, not always.
It's a choice that we must make.
Will I chose to harbor anger
Or let go, for Jesus' sake?

> And be ye kind one to another, tenderhearted, forgiving one another, even as God for Christ's sake hath forgiven you. (Ephesians 4:32)

> And when ye stand praying, forgive, if ye have ought against any: that your Father also which is in heaven may forgive you your trespasses. (Mark 11:25)

> If we confess our sins, he is faithful and just to forgive us [our] sins, and to cleanse us from all unrighteousness. (1 John 1:9)

> But if ye forgive not men their trespasses, neither will your Father forgive your trespasses. (Matthew 6:15)

> Then came Peter to him, and said, Lord, how oft shall my brother sin against me, and I forgive him? till seven times? (Matthew 18:21–22)

JUSTICE

Oh, justice, tell me—where does freedom lie?
Does it rest within the soul more bold than I?
Can I but know such fearless confidence
As to need no wall nor plan of self-defense?

Calm assurance of the soul I have not found
In the stilling of the barking hound.
Where is the victor's thrill of overcoming
The accuser's trepidations by succumbing?

To the stronghold of self-doubt and compromise,
Not a fortress but a dungeon in disguise,
The ceasing of the proud, condemning tongue
Comes but when psalms of praise to God are sung.

Then my spirit lifted high will doubtless soar
On freedom's golden wings forevermore.
In the distance, through the eyes of faith I see
The hand of justice bars the gates; grace holds the key.

> Learn to do well; seek judgment, relieve the oppressed, judge the fatherless, plead for the widow. (Isaiah 1:17)

> Thus speaketh the LORD of hosts, saying, Execute true judgment, and shew mercy and compassions every man to his brother: (Zechariah 7:9–10)

> Open thy mouth, judge righteously, and plead the cause of the poor and needy. (Jeremiah 22:3)

Thus saith the LORD; Execute ye judgment and righteousness, and deliver the spoiled out of the hand of the oppressor: and do no wrong, do no violence to the stranger, the fatherless, nor the widow, neither shed innocent blood in this place. (Proverbs 31:9)

Rejoice with them that do rejoice, and weep with them that weep. (Romans 12:15-18)

He hath shewed thee, O man, what [is] good; and what doth the LORD require of thee, but to do justly, and to love mercy, and to walk humbly with thy God? (Micah 6:8)

LEAVING

Life is fleeting; what care I
If tomorrow I may die?
Would I fast to this life cling?
Could I change a single thing?

Could I leave without regret?
I believe I could, and yet,
Thoughts of loved ones left behind
Cleave steadfastly to my mind.

Leaving without sweet good-bye;
Sometimes we must, but if not, why?
I'll take the time I have today
To tell them all I'd like to say.

So that all the words I've left unsaid,
Or, long forgotten, can be read.
Without reserve I shall impart
A lifetime of love into each heart

And say, throughout eternity,
Dear ones, when you remember me,
Know that before I bid adieu,
That my last thoughts were of loving you.

> Beloved, let us love one another: for love is of God; and every one that loveth is born of God, and knoweth God. (1 John 4:7–10)

[Be] kindly affectioned one to another with brotherly love; in honour preferring one another; (Romans 12:10)

My little children, let us not love in word, neither in tongue; but in deed and in truth. (1 John 3:18)

And as ye would that men should do to you, do ye also to them likewise. (Luke 6:31)

Beloved, if God so loved us, we ought also to love one another. (1 John 4:11)

Limelight

Oh, the thrilling ecstasy,
How marvelously sublime
To be walking in the light
And especially the lime.

There's no feeling on earth like it;
No sensation can compare
To the loftiness of limelight;
It's like floating on the air.

Limelight has a way of causing
Modesty to disappear.
Pride becomes a mark of honor,
Flattery a thing to cheer.

There's a subtle transformation
That occurs, without a doubt.
Inhibitions fade away
When the crowd begins to shout.

Whether minister or movie star,
Limelight works on both the same.
Green elixir, self-deceiving,
Sweet, intoxicating fame.

It's delicious to the ego,
Puffing up the mind and soul.
So consuming and addictive,
It caused Satan's head to roll.

So before you step out in it,
Let me give you this one clue:
If an angel couldn't take it,
What would limelight do to you?

> But the LORD said unto Samuel, Look not on his countenance, or on the height of his stature; because I have refused him: for [the LORD seeth] not as man seeth; for man looketh on the outward appearance, but the LORD looketh on the heart. (1 Samuel 16:7)
>
> Turn away mine eyes from beholding vanity; [and] quicken thou me in thy way. (Psalms 119:37)
>
> Favour [is] deceitful, and beauty [is] vain: [but] a woman [that] feareth the LORD, she shall be praised. (Proverbs 31:30)

Then I looked on all the works that my hands had wrought, and on the labour that I had laboured to do: and, behold, all [was] vanity and vexation of spirit and [there was] no profit under the sun. (Ecclesiastes 2:11)

He that loveth silver shall not be satisfied with silver; nor he that loveth abundance with increase: this [is] also vanity. (Ecclesiastes 5:10)

A man to whom God hath given riches, wealth, and honour, so that he wanteth nothing for his soul of all that he desireth, yet God giveth him not power to eat thereof, but a stranger eateth it: this [is] vanity, and it [is] an evil disease. (Ecclesiastes 6:2)

And [when] thou [art] spoiled, what wilt thou do? Though thou clothest thyself with crimson, though thou deckest thee with ornaments of gold, though thou rentest thy face with painting, in vain shalt thou make thyself fair; [thy] lovers will despise thee, they will seek thy life. (Jeremiah 4:30)

Humble yourselves therefore under the mighty hand of God that He may exalt you in due time. (1 Peter 5:6)

Light Sensitive

Listen to the sound of light
Ascending through the air,
Piercing shadows of the night;
'Tis the intercessor's prayer.

See the golden chords arise,
Iridescent holy rays,
Notes resounding to the skies;
'Tis the melody of praise.

Smell the fragrance sweetly gifted,
Hymns of glory softly sung,
Incense to the Father lifted,
By the power of the tongue.

Taste the goodness of the bread
God has provided for His own.
Children of the Lord are fed
Manna from the Father's throne.

Touch and feel the presence of
The Holy Spirit, manifest.
'Tis by the acquiescence of
The will of man in God at rest.

> I exhort therefore, that, first of all, supplications, prayers, intercessions, [and] giving of thanks, be made for all men; (1 Timothy 2:1)

Likewise the Spirit also helpeth our infirmities: for we know not what we should pray for as we ought: but the Spirit itself maketh intercession for us with groanings which cannot be uttered. (Romans 8:26)

Again I say unto you, That if two of you shall agree on earth as touching any thing that they shall ask, it shall be done for them of my Father which is in heaven. (Matthew 18:19–20)

Is any among you afflicted? let him pray. Is any merry? let him sing psalms. (James 5:13–16)

Praying always with all prayer and supplication in the Spirit, and watching thereunto with all perseverance and supplication for all saints; (Ephesians 6:18)

My Cross

When it seemed the world around me
Pressed in tight on every side,
When despair and heart aches
Seemed to surge like ocean tide,

I sat wondering in amazement,
How did this happen and why?
Does my God no longer answer?
Why did He not hear my cry?

Where and how have I departed
From the paths of joy and peace?
Have I not sought Him daily?
Have my prayers begun to cease?

Surely I had come to know
The joy His presence brings;
I had tasted of the new wine,
I had rested 'neath His wings.

How did I come to be so blind
While I prayed so diligently,
As I read the promises of His word,
And cried, At last I see!

In His love and tender mercy,
God has watched so patiently
As I wove my web in ignorance
And believed that I was free.

Free to fully live at last,
Abundant life, the Father's will.
No longer would I have to face
The pain of sin, Golgotha Hill.

I had arrived, or so I thought.
I was destined, don't you see?
To become a fearless warrior,
Born to set the captives free.

I fought battle after battle
Without thought of compromise.
Knowing when the war was over,
The conqueror would gain the prize.

Daily I secured my armor,
Daily I took up my sword,
While proclaiming victory
In the power of the Lord.

While my heart sang songs of praises
To my Lord whom I adore,
I neglected to take up the cross
That for me He gladly bore.

I cannot explain the miracle;
I only know the loss,
As the weight of all my burdens fell
When I took up my cross.

> And he said to them all If any man will come after me let him deny himself and take up his cross daily and follow me. (Luke 9:23)

For the preaching of the cross is to them that perish foolishness; but unto us which are saved it is the power of God. (1 Corinthians 1:18)

I want to know Christ and the power of his resurrection and the fellowship of sharing in his sufferings, becoming like him in his death, and so, somehow, to attain to the resurrection from the dead. Not that I have already obtained all this, or have already been made perfect. But I press on to take hold of that for which Christ Jesus took hold of me. (Philippians 3:10–12)

But we see Jesus, who was made a little lower than the angels, now crowned with glory and honor because he suffered death, so that by the grace of God he might taste death for everyone. (Hebrews 2:9)

My Mark

'Tis not upon the shifting sand
Where wind and tides erase
Inscriptions of this finite hand
That I with pen embrace.

The treasures of eternal bliss
Within the human soul
Where truth and mercy meet and kiss;
My heart becomes the scroll.

Interpreting each lovely word
Aglow with heaven's spark,
When by the Spirit I am stirred
And rise to make my mark.

Upon the tablet and I see
The hand of God in print;
Where God has made His mark on me,
Revealing His intent.

> A man's heart deviseth his way: but the LORD directeth his steps. (Proverbs 16:9)
>
> For we are his workmanship, created in Christ Jesus unto good works, which God hath before ordained that we should walk in them. (Ephesians 2:10)
>
> Therefore I say unto you, Take no thought for your life, what ye shall eat, or what ye shall drink; nor yet for your body, what ye shall put on. Is not the

life more than meat, and the body than raiment? (Matthew 6:25–34)

Before I formed thee in the belly I knew thee; and before thou camest forth out of the womb I sanctified thee, [and] I ordained thee a prophet unto the nations. (Jeremiah 1:5)

[There are] many devices in a man's heart; nevertheless the counsel of the LORD, that shall stand. (Proverbs 19:21)

My Preference

I've often thought of precepts taught
That foster consternation
As strangely odd, not sent from God,
But man's imagination.

I'd rather muse upon healthier views
Of sunlit skies and laughter,
And live each day in such a way
That joy shall follow after.

While some may insist on a negative twist,
Pessimistic in every opinion,
Still, the half-empty cup they refuse to fill up
Is the product of poverty's minion.

I'd much rather be the one people see
Who stops to smell the roses,
Never ceasing to share God's provision and care
And the riches His garden discloses.

I cannot speak for those who seek
To gain self-righteous pleasure
Through finding fault and rubbing salt
On the open wounds of God's treasure.

I'd rather be used to comfort the bruised
And to bind up the hearts that are broken
Than to prove I am right by the laws I recite,
Leaving words that are healing unspoken.

I cannot see, for the life of me,
How the gifts of God should be wasted
By the follies of guilt or the arguments built
Over wine that has never been tasted.

I'd much prefer my thoughts to stir
Such sparks as hope and beauty,
Than grit my teeth and strive beneath
The weight of pious duty.

Whether by chance or through circumstance,
Life has its problems, I know.
But I'd rather take heart, God's love to impart,
Than to say, I told you so.

As a child of the light, I have focused my sight
On the Lord; I choose no other reference.
Every thought finds its course, every mind its own source,
But the Spirit of God is my preference.

Therefore, brethren, stand fast, and hold the traditions which ye have been taught, whether by word, or our epistle. (2 Thessalonians 2:15)

Beware lest any man spoil you through philosophy and vain deceit, after the tradition of men, after the rudiments of the world, and not after Christ. (Colossians 2:8)

Preach the word; be instant in season, out of season; reprove, rebuke, exhort with all longsuffering and doctrine. (2 Timothy 4:2–4)

No Applause

He died alone;
No one truly understood the cause.
There was not one to give Him grateful praise,
No glory, no applause.

Did God expect
Anyone to recognize His valiant Son?
Not one soul who saw Him die could truly see
The battle fought, the victory won.

Was there a friend?
Was there anyone who stood up in the crowd
To honor Him? There was not one voice raised.
No one hailed Him, no one bowed.

He was accused.
They mocked Him, and they spat upon His face
"If he's the Christ then let him save himself."
Jesus died in disgrace.

No gratitude.
No thanks, nor was there any pity.
There was no sign of great appreciation
In Jerusalem, the holy city.

No sound of trumpets.
There was no heavenly host of angels singing,
Only ridicule and cruel jesting,
Mocking mouths, curses ringing.

What did He gain?
If not for glory, then why did He die?
We were the joy His Father set before Him,
The sin of man to crucify.

And what of those
Who have come to know that He is Lord?
Are we to seek to gain the praise of men?
Shall man's applause be our reward?

God forbid!
For the servant shall not be above his master,
And as surely as we gain the world's esteem,
Pride guarantees our own disaster.

So let us bow
In true humility before the God of grace.
In due time we shall receive the Lord's applause,
When we see Him in His glory, face to face

> I have been crucified with Christ. It is no longer I who live, but Christ who lives in me. And the life I now live in the flesh I live by faith in the Son of God, who loved me and gave himself for me. (Galatians 2:20)
>
> Therefore, since we have been justified by faith, we have peace with God through our Lord Jesus Christ. Through him we have also obtained access by faith into this grace in which we stand, and we rejoice in hope of the glory of God. More than that, we rejoice in our sufferings, knowing that suffering produces endurance, and endurance produces character, and character produces hope, and hope does not put us

to shame, because God's love has been poured into our hearts through the Holy Spirit who has been given to us. (Romans 5:1–21)

If we confess our sins, he is faithful and just to forgive us our sins and to cleanse us from all unrighteousness. (1 John 1:9)

Create in me a clean heart, O God, and renew a right spirit within me. Cast me not away from your presence, and take not your Holy Spirit from me. Restore to me the joy of your salvation, and uphold me with a willing spirit. (Psalm 51:10–12)

Beloved, we are God's children now, and what we will be has not yet appeared; but we know that when he appears we shall be like him, because we shall see him as he is. And everyone who thus hopes in him purifies himself as he is pure. (1 John 3:2–3)

One Small Boy

There was a time when I questioned
The reality of my Lord.
There was a time of uncertainty
When life was filled with discord.

Foolishly, I had turned away
And forsaken the God of my youth.
And in search for self-satisfaction,
I had lost all desire for the truth.

It is written that even a simple fool
Is right in his own eyes.
How can he trust and believe the word
Of a God whom he denies?

For you see, if we acknowledge
That His every word is true,
Then we must live accordingly,
And that, I refused to do.

Then in absolute desperation,
I cried out to Him in my pain.
I had nothing at all to lose but pride
And one small boy's life to gain.

But the God of my childhood heard my cries
And filled my soul with such joy
As He touched and healed the precious life
Of one small baby boy.

How could I ever doubt God's love,
His great mercy and His grace,
When day after day the joy is renewed
As I look upon Shane's face.

I marvel at the perfection
Of each tiny feature, and then
I remember and shudder to think of how
Without God, it would have been.

He came into this world too soon,
And so tiny he looked like a toy.
But God made a way where there was no way
For one small baby boy.

On our knees we knelt and prayed,
And as the hours passed,
We read the promises in God's word,
Then came the news at last.

A miracle! It was impossible!
He was dead, but now the child lives!
And all the glory be to God
For the life that the Father God gives!

How can I place my trust in God
And take Him at His word?
Because I've put Him to the test
And all my prayers, He's heard.

God heard my prayers and answered
With such tenderness and joy,
For as great as He is, He reached down and touched
One small baby boy.

This is the true story of my youngest son Shane. He was born prematurely, with too many life-threatening problems to mention. Two thirds of the way through a blood transfer, Shane actually died. He had cardiac arrest and was without any vital signs long enough to have done severe brain damage. In the natural, there was no hope for him to survive. Two weeks later, I was able to bring him home. He still weighed less than five pounds, but he was absolutely free of any residual effects, and he was completely healed.

Today, Shane is a very handsome, grown man. He's a healthy, whole six feet and two inch, two hundred-plus pound miracle. He is a gifted musician and sound technician. His full-time day gig is in the oil and gas industry as a corporate recruiter.

He loves the Lord, believes God's word, and is still a great joy to his mother.

> Bless the LORD, O my soul: and all that is within me, bless his holy name. Bless the LORD, O my soul, and forget not all his benefits: Who forgiveth all thine iniquities; who healeth all thy diseases; Who redeemeth thy life from destruction; who crowneth thee with lovingkindness and tender mercies; (Psalm 103)

On Paper

What are the words that I must write?
To quickly pen, lest I lose sight
Of answers given in the night.

Of dreams and visions clearly seen
Thoughts that flow so sweet and clean
That I in awe toward them lean.

To grasp each wondrous sight and sound
Of joy, where peace and love abound,
The splendor of such hallowed ground.

Could I but capture in my mind
As to within my memory bind,
That which daybreak leaves behind.

Oh, how can I begin to phrase
The message that such love conveys,
The excellence of all God's ways?

It was a dream, yet I confess
By knowing I am nonetheless
So overwhelmed that I must press.

With pen in hand upon the page,
And thus I now my heart engage,
The opening of heaven's stage.

In bold display of holy light,
Touching heaven as I write,
Becomes my gift and God's delight.

> Every good gift and every perfect gift is from above, and cometh down from the Father of lights, with whom is no variableness, neither shadow of turning. (James 1:17)
>
> My heart is inditing a good matter: I speak of the things which I have made touching the king: my tongue is the pen of a ready writer. Thou art fairer than the children of men: grace is poured into thy lips: therefore God hath blessed thee for ever. (Psalm 45:1–2)

Resurrection Power

Behold the majesty of our God,
Shout praises to our King!
Sing hosanna to the creator of life,
As He ushers in the spring.

The cold gray winter is over,
And bursting from its shroud
Comes the glory of resurrection power;
Death to life once more has bowed.

Fountains of crystal-clear water
Replenish the lifeless streams.
The melting snow rushes to join them
Cascading 'neath golden sunbeams.

The mountains rejoice, the little hills sing
As they don their new apparel.
The valleys shout, He has done a great thing!
Maranatha! the deserts herald.

He has clothed the earth with splendor,
The scent of jasmine fills the air,
The Rose of Sharon blossoms
By the delicate maiden's hair.

Fairer than all His creation
Crowned with glory and with grace,
With His beauty He now surrounds us
And robes the earth in emerald lace.

Out of the ivory palaces,
He comes to take His own.
All rise as He takes the hand of His bride
And leads her to heaven's throne.

> The voice of my beloved! behold, he cometh leaping upon the mountains, skipping upon the hills.
>
> My beloved is like a roe or a young hart: behold, he standeth behind our wall, he looketh forth at the windows, shewing himself through the lattice.
>
> My beloved spake, and said unto me, Rise up, my love, my fair one, and come away.
>
> For, lo, the winter is past, the rain is over and gone;

The flowers appear on the earth; the time of the singing of birds is come, and the voice of the turtle is heard in our land;

The fig tree putteth forth her green figs, and the vines with the tender grape give a good smell. Arise, my love, my fair one, and come away.

O my dove, that art in the clefts of the rock, in the secret places of the stairs, let me see thy countenance, let me hear thy voice; for sweet is thy voice, and thy countenance is comely.

Take us the foxes, the little foxes, that spoil the vines: for our vines have tender grapes.

My beloved is mine, and I am his: he feedeth among the lilies.

Until the day break, and the shadows flee away, turn, my beloved, and be thou like a roe or a young hart upon the mountains of Bether. (Song of Solomon 2:8–17)

Sharing Life

Lord Jesus, have your way today
Within this heart of mine,
And as I live my life, dear Lord,
Help me live it as though it were Thine.

So anxious are your children, Lord,
To call upon Your name,
When trials and grief and heartaches come
Or the heat of affliction's flame.

We need You so, our burdens to bear,
In times of despair and depression,
And we cling to each precious promise You made
During famine and flood and recession.

But when times are good and storehouses are full,
When we're prosperous and we're healthy,
Do we spend as much time on our knees in prayer
As we did before we were wealthy?

And are we so anxious to share with You
On the mountains of triumph and gladness
As we were to share our sorrows and shame
Through the valleys of fear and sadness?

Ashamedly, Lord, I must confess,
That so often we ignore You.
We're so involved with living our lives
That we let other things come before You.

Why must we wait for troubled times,
When we're burdened down with care,
Before we turn our heart toward You
And kneel before You in prayer?

Perhaps I've come to realize
How selfish and thoughtless and vain
I would consider a friend who shared
Only troubles and sorrows and pain.

And so I humbly ask You, Lord,
To share throughout all my years
Each moment of the life I live,
All my laughter as well as my tears.

> When thou hast eaten and art full, then thou shalt bless the Lord thy God for the good land which he hath given thee.
>
> Beware that thou forget not the Lord thy God, in not keeping his commandments, and his judgments, and his statutes, which I command thee this day:
>
> Lest when thou hast eaten and art full, and hast built goodly houses, and dwelt therein;
>
> And when thy herds and thy flocks multiply, and thy silver and thy gold is multiplied, and all that thou hast is multiplied;
>
> Then thine heart be lifted up, and thou forget the Lord thy God, which brought thee forth out of the land of Egypt, from the house of bondage;
> (Deuteronomy 8:10–14)

Sunday Morning Sunrise

Breezes still, morning chill,
Dewdrops cover pale green leaves,
Stirring sounds above the grounds,
Misty shadows gently cleave.

Daughters fair, grief forbear,
Journey to their Savior's tomb.
Before daybreak, aloes take,
Mourners through the shadows' gloom .

Holy stones, sacred tones,
Giant boulder rolled away.
Borrowed cave, empty grave,
Where Christ's lifeless body lay.

Drawing near, trembling fear;
Where could they have taken Him?
Why weepest thou? Whom seeketh thou?
The Living Word said unto them.

Love enfolding, now beholding,
Falling at the Master's feet.
All transcending, Christ ascending,
Heaven's mission now complete.

Sunrise, eastern skies,
Heaven's seraph witnessing;
Angelic voice in awe rejoice,
All Glory to the risen King.

In the end of the sabbath, as it began to dawn toward the first day of the week, came Mary Magdalene and the other Mary to see the sepulchre. And, behold, there was a great earthquake: for the angel of the Lord descended from heaven, and came and rolled back the stone from the door, and sat upon it. His countenance was like lightning, and his raiment white as snow: And for fear of him the keepers did shake, and became as dead men. And the angel answered and said unto the women, Fear not ye: for I know that ye seek Jesus, which was crucified. He is not here: for he is risen, as he said. Come, see the place where the Lord lay. And go quickly, and tell his disciples that he is risen from the dead; and, behold, he goeth before you into Galilee; there shall ye see him: lo, I have told you. (Matthew 28:1–7)

The Day

It was a day, an unholy day,
When darkness withstood the divine,
And white clouds turned to charcoal gray
As the sun refused to shine.

It was a day, an unholy day,
When all hope for humanity died,
For darkness increased in evil display
When our Savior was crucified.

It was a day, an unholy day,
When the earth's convulsing sod
Quaked and trembled in utter dismay
'Neath the blood of the Son of God.

It was a day, an unholy day,
When the temple veil was rent
By the breath of heaven in such a way
That no power on earth could prevent.

It was a day, an unholy day,
Oh, but look what the Father has done!
In the midst of the darkness, God made a way
For the light to come forth in His Son.

Oh, yes, it was a day, a glorious day,
When God paid the ultimate price,
And the light of the world still shines today
In heaven's sacrifice.

Arise, shine; for thy light is come, and the glory of the LORD is risen upon thee. For, behold, the darkness shall cover the earth, and gross darkness the people: but the LORD shall arise upon thee, and his glory shall be seen upon thee. And the Gentiles shall come to thy light, and kings to the brightness of thy rising. (Isaiah 60:1–3)

Now from the sixth hour there was darkness over all the land unto the ninth hour.

And about the ninth hour Jesus cried with a loud voice, saying, Eli, Eli, lama sabachthani? that is to say, My God, my God, why hast thou forsaken me? Some of them that stood there, when they heard that, said, This man calleth for Elias. And straightway one of them ran, and took a spunge, and filled it with vinegar, and put it on a reed, and gave him to drink. The rest said, Let be, let us see whether Elias will come to save him. Jesus, when he had cried again with a loud voice, yielded up the ghost. And, behold, the veil of the temple was rent in twain from the top to the bottom; and the earth did quake, and the rocks rent; And the graves were opened; and many bodies of the saints which slept arose, And came out of the graves after his resurrection, and went into the holy city, and appeared unto many. Now when the centurion, and they that were with him, watching Jesus, saw the earthquake, and those things that were done, they feared greatly, saying, Truly this was the Son of God. (Matthew 27:45–54)

The Holy One

Oh Holy One, I lift my eyes
To look beyond earth's troubled skies.

I see the Son, and through the haze
His glory shines, His eyes ablaze,

With light and laughter, love and grace
Proceeding from His wondrous face.

Without a sound nor spoken word,
How is it, Lord, that I have heard

And understand such glorious things,
That peace and joy within me springs?

He opened not His mouth to speak,
But in radiant mystique,

The Holy One revealed to me
That which mere eyes could never see.

The Living Word, the great I Am,
God incarnate, perfect lamb,

Who is and was before all time,
Deity with gaze sublime,

Has looked down from heaven's throne,
All glorious His visage shown.

In manifested brilliance rare,
I looked to Him and found Him there,

And stand in awe remembering
The love of God in Christ, my King.

> But one in a certain place testified, saying, What is man, that thou art mindful of him? or the son of man, that thou visitest him? Thou madest him a little lower than the angels; thou crownedst him with glory and honour, and didst set him over the works of thy hands: Thou hast put all things in subjection under his feet. For in that he put all in subjection under him, he left nothing *that is* not put under him. But now we see not yet all things put under him. (Hebrews 2:6–8)

> Behold, he cometh with clouds; and every eye shall see him, and they also which pierced him: and all

kindreds of the earth shall wail because of him. Even so, Amen. And I turned to see the voice that spake with me. And being turned, I saw seven golden candlesticks; And in the midst of the seven candlesticks one like unto the Son of man, clothed with a garment down to the foot, and girt about the paps with a golden girdle. His head and his hairs were white like wool, as white as snow; and his eyes were as a flame of fire; And his feet like unto fine brass, as if they burned in a furnace; and his voice as the sound of many waters. And he had in his right hand seven stars: and out of his mouth went a sharp two-edged sword: and his countenance was as the sun shineth in his strength. And when I saw him, I fell at his feet as dead. And he laid his right hand upon me, saying unto me, Fear not; I am the first and the last: I am he that liveth, and was dead; and, behold, I am alive for evermore, Amen; and have the keys of hell and of death. Write the things which thou hast seen, and the things which are, and the things which shall be hereafter; (Revelation 1:7, 12–19)

The Lost Sheep

A lifetime ago, at ten years old,
I caught a glimpse of glory
As I sat in a tiny, white, country church
And heard the gospel story.

How my young heart thrilled to hear
Of the Savior from Galilee,
Who was born in the manger of Bethlehem
And died to set me free.

I believed in the strong and humble man
And received Him as my Lord.
The carpenter who was God in man,
I worshipped and adored.

But the heart and mind of a simple child,
Uncluttered by pride and doubt,
Fell prey to the trappings of the world
As I learned what the world was about.

And so, alas, in my late teens,
I joined another crowd.
From the gentle shepherd I turned away
To run with the arrogant and the proud.

Painful were the many years
That I spent away from my Lord,
As I struggled through the grief and tears
Losing faith in treasures I had stored.

Faithful is the Great Shepherd
Who, whenever a lamb goes astray,
Will search for her to the ends of the earth
And mercifully teach her to obey.

To follow the Master carefully,
Trusting in His love and care,
As He leads His flock to green pastures
To drink from the still waters there.

He rescued me from the wilderness,
From the briars that entangled me there,
From the mouths of angry wolves,
And the tempter's deadly snare.

He has given me joy in the morning,
In my heart He has placed a new song.
For His goodness and His tender mercies
Shall follow me all my life long.

I bow my knee to the Shepherd of love,
The Christ of the age-old story;
For the great good news to all mankind
Is Jesus, the King of all glory.

> Lift up your heads, O ye gates; and be ye lift up, ye everlasting doors; and the King of glory shall come in. Who is this King of glory? The LORD strong and mighty, the LORD mighty in battle. Lift up your heads, O ye gates; even lift them up, ye everlasting doors; and the King of glory shall come in. Who is this King of glory? The LORD of hosts, he is the King of glory. Selah. (Psalm 24:7–10)

The Lamb's Prayer

Gentle Shepherd, lead me,
Lest I be tempted to hide
Your gospel for rear of ridicule,
To protect my foolish pride.

And, Lord, I pray You'll remind me
When I have an occasion to speak,
Never to judge another lamb
Who appears to be doubtful and weak.

Remind me, Lord, when others deny
Your word and reject it as truth,
That I, too, fell prey to unbelief
And strayed from the God of my youth.

I was lost, but my Shepherd found me,
Wandering aimlessly out in the cold,
When You lifted me with arms of love
And carried me back to the fold.

No words of condemnation fell
Upon these grateful ears,
But cleansing floods of mercy flowed
And washed away my fears.

The King of love my Shepherd is,
Oh, yes, and so much more;
The Lamb of God, for sinners slain,
Himself has become the door.

And welcome are the sheep who stray
To join the Shepherd, if you will,
To walk with Him in pastures green,
By waters clear and still.

And you shall learn the Lamb's prayer
As your souls are being restored
In the likeness of the Lamb of God
And the goodness of the Lord.

Fill our hearts with your compassion,
Not speaking our own word but thine,
And through all the dear sheep of your pasture
Let the light of the Great Shepherd shine.

> The LORD is my shepherd; I shall not want. He maketh me to lie down in green pastures: he leadeth me beside the still waters. He restoreth my soul: he leadeth me in the paths of righteousness for his name's sake. Yea, though I walk through the valley of the shadow of death, I will fear no evil: for thou art with me; thy rod and thy staff they comfort me. Thou preparest a table before me in the presence of mine enemies: thou anointest my head with oil; my cup runneth over. (Psalm 23:1–5)

The Mystery

The mystery unravels
As we journey on our way,
And in all our earthly travels,
We are guided day by day.

Our destiny is certain,
Our eternal home secure,
far beyond the velvet curtain
Beckoning with sweet allure.

So often roads are hidden,
Some pathways run parallel,
Lined by trees with fruit forbidden,
Yet by sight one cannot tell.

It is only by the hearing
Of the Master's still, small voice
That we recognize the clearing
Of the road that is His choice.

And the mystery unfolding
Now before these earthly eyes
Is the treasure we are holding
As we run to gain the prize.

Flesh can't understand the story,
It sounds too good to be true;
Christ is now the hope of glory,
Not in heaven, but in you.

And you, that were sometime alienated and enemies in your mind by wicked works, yet now hath he reconciled in the body of his flesh through death, to present you holy and unblameable and unreproveable in his sight: If ye continue in the faith grounded and settled, and be not moved away from the hope of the gospel, which ye have heard, and which was preached to every creature which is under heaven; whereof I Paul am made a minister; Who now rejoice in my sufferings for you, and fill up that which is behind of the afflictions of Christ in my flesh for his body's sake, which is the church: Whereof I am made a minister, according to the dispensation of God which is given to me for you, to fulfil the word of God; Even the mystery which hath been hid from ages and from generations, but now is made manifest to his saints: To whom God would make known what is the riches of the glory of this mystery among the Gentiles; which is Christ in you, the hope of glory: (Colossians 1:21–27)

The Nativity

There were no snowflakes falling on that silent, holy night,
No jingle bells in Israel nor candles shining bright.
There was no Santa Clause or reindeer anywhere in sight,
And Rudolph's nose, as some suppose, was not the guiding light.

No mistletoe was hanging high above the shepherds' heads.
No sugarplums, no little toy drums, no icicles or sleds.
No one was dreaming of candy canes or gumdrops or gingerbread,
But in absolute awe the shepherds saw the angels on high instead.

No one saw the shining star but for the wise men sent,
And there were few of those who knew just what the prophets meant.
Concerning the birth of a baby boy in Bethlehem, no acknowledgment,
No church bells rang, but the angels sang of this glorious event.

His birthplace a small, stone shelter, a cave where animals stay.
In the cold of the night, without heat or light, the baby Jesus lay.
No soft, warm blankets, but swaddling clothes
    Mary wrapped Him in that day.
Without cradle or bed, Joseph fashioned instead
    a place for God's Son on the hay.

Every house was dark in Bethlehem town
    and in all the streets thereof.
All were sleeping while angels were keeping
    their watch of wondrous love.
Did the Spirit of God accompany the Son in
    the form of a pure white dove
On that glorious night when heaven's great
    light shone from the heavens above?

Did He cry when the baby Jesus was born? Did
    He know from whence he came?
Were there memories stored in the heart of the Lord?
    Did He know He would carry our shame?
Did He understand as a tiny babe that He would take the blame
For the sins of mankind? What was in His
    mind when God incarnate became?

No, oh, no, there could be no thoughts
    within the Christ child's mind;
When the Great I am became a man, He
    left all heaven's glory behind.
This newborn babe had chosen to come to
    give sight to all who were blind,
For the blessed Christ child was reconciled to
    become the savior of all mankind.

And so it was that the Word of God was made
    manifest on that first Christmas morn:
No red velvet gown, no golden crown by
    the King of Kings was worn.
But with glory and splendor and pure holy
    light did the Bethlehem Star adorn
The sweet spotless Lamb, son of Abraham, on the
    day that Jesus our Savior was born.

> And it came to pass in those days, that there went out a decree from Caesar Augustus that all the world should be taxed. (And this taxing was first made when Cyrenius was governor of Syria.) And all went to be taxed, every one into his own city. And Joseph also went up from Galilee, out of the city of Nazareth, into Judaea, unto the city of David, which is called Bethlehem; (because he was of the house and lineage of David:) To be taxed with Mary his espoused wife, being great with child. And so it was, that, while they were there, the days were accomplished that she should be delivered. And she brought forth her firstborn son, and wrapped him in swaddling clothes, and laid him in a manger; because there was no room for them in the inn. And there were in the same country shepherds abiding in the field, keeping watch over their flock by night. And, lo, the angel of the Lord came upon them, and the glory of the Lord shone round about them: and they were sore afraid. And the angel said unto them, Fear not: for, behold, I bring you good tidings of great joy, which shall be to all people. For unto you is born this day in the city of David a Saviour, which is Christ the Lord. And this shall be a sign unto you; Ye shall find the babe wrapped in

swaddling clothes, lying in a manger. And suddenly there was with the angel a multitude of the heavenly host praising God, and saying, Glory to God in the highest, and on earth peace, good will toward men. (Luke 2:1–14)

The Real Jesus

For all things genuine and true,
They say there is a counterfeit.
For every imitator's skew,
There lies the slant of a hypocrite.

Sometimes it's difficult to tell
The real thing from the substitute,
But those who know the vintner well
Will also recognize his fruit.

And so it is for those who bear
The Lord's resemblance and are real;
The proof is not the cross they wear,
But in the Holy Spirit's seal.

'Tis not a mark that can be seen
Nor attitudes that we reflect.
Only God can judge between
Some pietists and His elect.

The earthen vessel's identity lies
Within the contents of each cup.
There is no need to advertise,
Will the real Jesus please stand up?

> Beware of false prophets, which come to you in sheep's clothing, but inwardly they are ravening wolves. Ye shall know them by their fruits. Do men gather grapes of thorns, or figs of thistles? Even so every good tree bringeth forth good fruit; but a

corrupt tree bringeth forth evil fruit. A good tree cannot bring forth evil fruit, neither can a corrupt tree bring forth good fruit. Every tree that bringeth not forth good fruit is hewn down, and cast into the fire. Wherefore by their fruits ye shall know them. (Matthew 7:15–20)

The Two-Edged Sword

The two-edged sword they could not wield;
'Twas for them but excess weight.
They had no use for blade nor shield,
Alas, until it was too late.

Fierce was the enemy and wise
In battle strategy and plan;
Wolves were they in sheep's disguise,
By nature, enemies of man.

"Divide and conquer," whispered they,
Beneath their cold and lifeless breath.
"We shall divide the saints today
And scatter them with words of death."

Quietly the ravening wolves did creep
Into the pews of the congregation,
Who neither shield nor weapons keep,
Nor helmets of salvation.

Demonic doctrines they did weave,
Strongholds of doubt and fear.
Twisting scriptures to deceive
Unsuspecting eyes and ears.

Undone by sudden loss of sight,
They had no strength to stand.
Blind were they without the light,
Snared by the enemy's cunning hand.

"The war is over, don't you see?
You cannot hope to win.
Forget your plans of victory,
You are all slaves to your sin.

"You are but fodder for hell's flames,
And we shall surely pierce your hearts.
Because you bear no shield of faith,
You shall not quench our fiery darts."

Then came forth a mighty sound
As the Lion of Judah roared,
And He put the enemy to flight
With his mighty two-edged sword.

Then said He to the captives freed,
"You are loosed from the bondage of fear.
The enemy shall not succeed."
And He bid them all draw near.

"Long have I waited patiently
For you, dear saints, to realize
The power of My word," said He,
"To put to naught the serpent's lies."

"The shield of faith you have refused.
Your robes are stained with pride and torn.
The sword of the Spirit you have not used.
Salvation's helmet you've not worn.

"Will you not take the gifts I give
To overcome the world at length?
To die to self that you might live
By faith and supernatural strength.

"I tell you, dear ones, if you reject
That which I offer you today,
I can neither shelter nor protect
Those who choose another way.

"I shall leave you now to make the choice;
Your decision determines your fate.
But those who choose to hear My voice,
True victory shall celebrate."

I stood and watched some walk away
And cried for their terrible loss.
Wolves disguised as sheep were they,
Despising the way of the cross.

> Behold, I send you forth as sheep in the midst of wolves: be ye therefore wise as serpents, and harmless as doves. (Matthew 10:16)
>
> Go your ways: behold, I send you forth as lambs among wolves, (Luke 10:3)
>
> For I know this, that after my departing shall grievous wolves enter in among you, not sparing the flock. (Acts 20:29)

The Watchman

Go and post a lookout. Let the watchman stand alert
To hear the sound of horses' hooves pounding in the dirt.

Let him stand in the tower to report all that he sees,
For the desert sands are shifting by the changing of the breeze.

An invader comes from the desert like a
    whirlwind sweeping through.
He is from the land of terror, and survivors will be few.

Tell the watchman he must shout, though the people will not hear,
And the warnings he will give shall not penetrate their ear.

They will say unto their leaders, "Raise the soldiers up to fight."
They will call unto the watchman, "What is left of the night?"

Day after day, the watchman will stand, steady at his post,
While the people eat and drink and of all their power boast.

"Watchman, Watchman, tell us when the enemy is in sight.
Until then we will not rise; we shall sleep through the night."

"The morning surely will come," the watchman then replies,
"But darkness now hangs heavenly upon the eastern skies.

"If you would ask then ask me, but come back yet again.
For I tell you it is certain that your asking is in vain."

"Watchman, Watchman, hold your tongue, it is not for you to say
That our questioning is pointless. We will surely have our way.

"So tell us now, dear watchman, what is left of the night?
Is the morning sun approaching? Is the glow of it in sight?

"We are tired of all the waiting, and of rumors we are leery.
Perhaps we've moved too quickly, for the soldiers now grow weary.

"We have called up every officer to arise and anoint the shield,
But how long must they remain standing on the battlefield?

"Watchman, Watchman, tell us." And the
    watchman answers back,
"Though the morning sun arises, the skies will still be black.

I see war on the horizon, fire and brimstone fill the air,
A dark and grievous vision," the watchman must declare.

"Therefore, now, my loins are filled with
    pain as a woman in travail.
Such pangs have taken hold of me, I fear my heart will fail.

"The enemy dealeth treacherously. He comes to take the spoil,
To plunder and pillage a nation, to seize the wealth and oil.

"His hands are stained with innocent blood,
    yet he stands in bold defiance
And proclaims that God is with him, as he boasts of his reliance."

"Watchman, Watchman, tell us, is he willing to discuss
A possible withdrawal? Surely he will listen to us.

"Is there not one possibility that we have not discovered?
Have we looked at every option? Is there any left uncovered?

The watchman cries out loudly, "I have stood both day and night!
I have not failed to warn you of the danger within sight.

"I have stood upon the tower. I have told you what I see.
I can neither change the vision nor withhold the prophecy.

"If you will not heed the warning nor listen to the trumpet sound
Then listen to the hoofbeats as they thunder on the ground.

"Look toward this far horizon. The shield has been anointed.
You cannot stop the desert storm or avoid
    what God has appointed.

"Watchman, Watchman, silence! Who asked you to prophesy?
We're not interested in your religion or the warnings in the sky.

"Now, Watchman, tell us plainly, make it accurate and clear.
Without all the innuendoes, tell us what we want to hear.

"Tell us when it will be over. Tell us how long this will last.
Is the morning now approaching? Will the darkness soon be past?"

And the watchman saw a chariot and two horses ridden by men,
A chariot of horses and camels, and harkened with diligence then.

And he cried out with a loud voice, "That
    which I have heard, I will speak.
But I warn you that the message is not the one you seek.

"Long after Babylon has fallen, the cry of war will sound,
Until all the images of its god lie shattered on the ground."

> Son of man, I have made thee a watchman unto the house of Israel: therefore hear the word at my mouth, and give them warning from me. (Ezekiel 3:17)
>
> I have set watchmen upon thy walls, O Jerusalem, [which] shall never hold their peace day nor night: ye that make mention of the LORD, keep not silence, (Isaiah 62:6)
>
> But if the watchman see the sword come, and blow not the trumpet, and the people be not warned; if the sword come, and take any person from among them, he is taken away in his iniquity; but his blood will I require at the watchman's hand. (Ezekiel 33:6)
>
> The burden of the desert of the sea. As whirlwinds in the south pass through; so it cometh from the desert, from a terrible land. A grievous vision is declared unto me; the treacherous dealer dealeth treacherously, and the spoiler spoileth. Go up, O Elam: besiege, O Media; all the sighing thereof have I made to cease. Therefore are my loins filled with pain: pangs have taken hold upon me, as the pangs

of a woman that travaileth: I was bowed down at the hearing of it; I was dismayed at the seeing of it. My heart panted, fearfulness affrighted me: the night of my pleasure hath he turned into fear unto me. Prepare the table, watch in the watchtower, eat, drink: arise, ye princes, and anoint the shield. For thus hath the Lord said unto me, Go, set a watchman, let him declare what he seeth. And he saw a chariot with a couple of horsemen, a chariot of asses, and a chariot of camels; and he hearkened diligently with much heed: And he cried, A lion: My lord, I stand continually upon the watchtower in the daytime, and I am set in my ward whole nights: And, behold, here cometh a chariot of men, with a couple of horsemen. And he answered and said, Babylon is fallen, is fallen; and all the graven images of her gods he hath broken unto the ground. (Isaiah 21:1–9)

Traveling Clothes

As I make my journey homeward, Lord,
How wonderful to know
That in sunshine or rain, You will remain,
While the seasons come and go.

And as winter's chill approaches,
And the sun slowly fades from view,
When my eyes close in death, and I breathe my last breath,
There's no shadow of changing with You.

I'll have no fear or grief in departing
From this world of sorrow and pain,
And though loved ones may weep, I know You will keep
Them safe 'til I see them again.

How sweet is the total assurance
Of your love and your grace toward me.
Through faith in the blood, the all-cleansing flood
Of the Christ of Calvary.

I have no other refuge, Lord,
I seek no other place of rest.
This one thing I know, when my time comes to go,
I shall be ready and dressed.

In a robe of fine, snow-white linen,
Pure and clean, without wrinkle or spot,
By Your hands tailor-made, and overlaid
With your mercy, and I shall fear not.

But until that day comes, precious Jesus,
When I meet you in heaven above,
As I dwell here below, may my faith in you show
To others your fathomless love.

> A new commandment I give unto you, That ye love one another; as I have loved you, that ye also love one another. (John 13:34)

> And I heard as it were the voice of a great multitude, and as the voice of many waters, and as the voice of mighty thunderings, saying, Alleluia: for the Lord God omnipotent reigneth. Let us be glad and rejoice, and give honour to him: for the marriage of the Lamb is come, and his wife hath made herself ready. And to her was granted that she should be arrayed in fine linen, clean and white: for the fine linen is the righteousness of saints. (Revelation 19:6–7)

WHAT HAS BEEN DONE

What has man done, in his own attempt
To fulfill God's laws, but confuse them?
What has man done, in his own attempt
To control God's sheep, but abuse them?

What has man done, in his own attempt
To gain God's favor, but miss it?
What has man done? He has not measured up,
For the standard of God is explicit.

What has man done? He has forfeited grace
For the works of self-justification.
What has man done? He has followed the course
Of his human imagination.

What has man done? He has chosen to eat
Of the tree in the midst of the garden.
What has man done? He has rationalized
Through reason his actions to pardon.

What has man done? He has taken the Word
Of the Lord in his mouth and reviled it.
What has man done? He has taken the bread
Of the Lord in his hands and defiled it.

What has God done? God has not changed,
His word abides forever.
What has God done? His mercy remains,
His goodness faileth never.

What has God done? In the flesh He has come,
In the form of His own creation.
What Has God done? With the blood of His Son
He has purchased man's salvation.

What has God done? He has fashioned a tree
In the shape of a rugged cross.
What has God done? He has poured out His life
To compensate for our loss.

What has God done? He took pity upon
This sinful human race.
God has overcome what man has done
By His sovereign, boundless grace.

> And you, that were sometime alienated and enemies in your mind by wicked works, yet now hath he reconciled In the body of his flesh through death, to present you holy and unblameable and unreproveable in his sight: If ye continue in the faith grounded and settled, and be not moved away from the hope of the gospel, which ye have heard, and which was preached to every creature which is under heaven; whereof I Paul am made a minister; Who now rejoice in my sufferings for you, and fill up that which is behind of the afflictions of Christ in my flesh for his body's sake, which is the church: Whereof I am made a minister, according to the dispensation of God which is given to me for you, to fulfil the word of God; Even the mystery which hath been hid from ages and from generations, but now is made manifest to his saints: To whom God would make known what is the riches of the glory of this mystery among the Gentiles; which is Christ in

you, the hope of glory: And no man hath ascended up to heaven, but he that came down from heaven, even the Son of man which is in heaven. [14] And as Moses lifted up the serpent in the wilderness, even so must the Son of man be lifted up: [5] That whosoever believeth in him should not perish, but have eternal life. (John 3:21–27)

For God so loved the world, that he gave his only begotten Son, that whosoever believeth in him should not perish, but have everlasting life. For God sent not his Son into the world to condemn the world; but that the world through him might be saved. (John 3:16–17)

WHAT WORKS

Profit netting, quota getting, special formulas and plans,
Magic keys, right recipes, God's ideas or man's,
Self-defending, goal tending, calculating cool endeavor,
Proper tools, rigid rules, mind control; how clever!

Get it right, set your sight on perfection, nothing less.
Do it this way, just like I say, and I guarantee success.
Persevere, it's simple, dear; utilize your gifts and talents.
Keep on climbing, watch your timing; careful
    now, maintain your balance.

Do your duty, see the beauty in the thorns and not the rose.
What's the purpose 'neath the surface? Pious nonsense, I suppose.
Religious voices offer choices (yours, they say, to make).
Others yell, "You'll go to hell!" if their man-made rules you break.

Old traditions, superstitions, scream defeat with every breath,
Fists pounding, judgment sounding, scare the sinners half to death.
Secret locks, God in a box, some contend without a doubt.
They maintain their hands contain the keys to let Him out.

Once saved, always saved, disagreement, strong debate,
Condemnation, lost salvation, denominational pearly gates.
Silly fables, turning tables, neither one is right
On the level of the devil, instigator of the fight.

Guilt, depression, soul confession, evil overcoming good.
Never ending, sentence pending, amazing grace misunderstood.
Sweet and sour, words empower, gossips carry tales.
Self-conviction, contradiction, love never fails.

Dogmatic mold, pigeon-holed, obligation mandatory;
Lord, I quit! I just don't fit into that category!
His restrictions, her predictions, accusations, repercussions.
What to do? Don't pursue argumentative discussions.

Wagging tongues, pride-filled lungs, mouths that love to talk
Delight to feed on sacred seed, but do not walk the walk.
Pointed fingers, sadness lingers, trying not to care.
Loss of hope, how to cope, feelings of despair.

Dry bones, living stones crushing one another.
Pole vaulting, self-exalting, brother against brother.
Where to go, I don't know; unproductive, endless search.
Universal saint's rehearsal, nonexistent perfect church.

Days elapse, unstructured perhaps, no qualms, no quibbles, no quirks.
With an attitude of gratitude, the prayer of faith still works.
Assembly forsaken? Foundation shaken? Wrong! Guess again!
I've still got my Lord and a two-edged sword; you lose, Devil, I win!

> There is therefore now no condemnation to them which are in Christ Jesus, who walk not after the flesh, but after the Spirit. For the law of the Spirit of life in Christ Jesus hath made me free from the law of sin and death. For what the law could not do, in that it was weak through the flesh, God sending his own Son in the likeness of sinful flesh, and for sin, condemned sin in the flesh: That the righteousness of the law might be fulfilled in us, who walk not after the flesh, but after the Spirit. For they that are after the flesh do mind the things of the flesh; but they that are after the Spirit the things of the Spirit. For to be carnally minded is death; but to be spiritually minded is life and peace. (Romans 8:1–6)

Wilderness

There is a place I must go through
Of necessity, not choice,
A desert place where trials subdue
The lifting of my voice.

A place where I can see no good,
Nor reason to exist,
Where heat and thirst must be withstood,
No refuge to assist.

No wellsprings flowing from within,
Nor evidence of green,
Tracks in the sand where I have been
And fallen in-between.

I see no pools beneath the skies
Nor clouds that promise rain.
The wilderness beyond me lies
In treacherous terrain.

I hear no sound of angels wings,
No guidance or direction.
I can't detect one single thing
To count on for protection.

Yet in the desert place I find
That which my eyes can't see.
It makes no difference when my mind
Is focused, Lord, on Thee.

And when it seems I've lost my way,
In hope I shall prevail.
It matters not what others say,
For my God cannot fail.

And I shall rise to praise my God,
Regardless of my pain,
For in the wilderness I see
The evidence of rain.

I'll walk by faith and not by sight
And in the desert boast:
'Tis not by power nor by might,
But by the Holy Ghost.

> So I answered and spake to the angel that talked with me, saying, What are these, my lord? Then the angel that talked with me answered and said unto me, Knowest thou not what these be? And

I said, No, my lord. Then he answered and spake unto me, saying, This is the word of the LORD unto Zerubbabel, saying, Not by might, nor by power, but by my spirit, saith the LORD of hosts. (Zechariah 4:4–6)

Then was Jesus led up of the Spirit into the wilderness to be tempted of the devil. And when he had fasted forty days and forty nights, he was afterward an hungred. And when the tempter came to him, he said, If thou be the Son of God, command that these stones be made bread. But he answered and said, It is written, Man shall not live by bread alone, but by every word that proceedeth out of the mouth of God. Then the devil taketh him up into the holy city, and setteth him on a pinnacle of the temple, And saith unto him, If thou be the Son of God, cast thyself down: for it is written, He shall give his angels charge concerning thee: and in their hands they shall bear thee up, lest at any time thou dash thy foot against a stone. Jesus said unto him, It is written again, Thou shalt not tempt the Lord thy God. Again, the devil taketh him up into an exceeding high mountain, and sheweth him all the kingdoms of the world, and the glory of them; And saith unto him, All these things will I give thee, if thou wilt fall down and worship me. Then saith Jesus unto him, Get thee hence, Satan: for it is written, Thou shalt worship the Lord thy God, and him only shalt thou serve. Then the devil leaveth him, and, behold, angels came and ministered unto him. (Matthew 4:1–11)

Will You Gamble

Will you gamble? Do you dare,
When you know in advance
That you will reap the seed you sow?
Why would you take that chance?

Are you prepared? Will you stand
On the sovereign word of God?
Have you girded the loins of your mind with truth?
Are your feet with the gospel shod?

Does the breastplate of righteousness cover your heart?
Is the salvation helmet in place?
Is the shield of faith quenching fiery darts
Of the wicked, erasing each trace?

Are you wielding the sword of the Spirit?
Is the Word of God on your tongue?
Are you opening the prison doors?
Have you broken the bars? Have the locks been sprung?

Or will you gamble? Do you dare?
Will you walk after fleshly desires?
When the way of the world seems pleasant,
Yielding is fuel to lust's fires.

Will you compromise when trials come,
When fear and terror assail you?
Will you dare to trust in God
For strength that will not fail you?

Yours is the freedom, yours the choice,
Yours the decision to make.
Will you live for self-gain and pleasure
When your very life is at stake?

Why would you choose to walk blindly,
Defying God's spiritual law,
When with open eyes you may clearly see
His glory in splendor and awe?

When you know His power and His love,
His abundant life and provision,
Why would you choose to walk in death?
Would you knowingly make that decision?

Also knowing that you will account
For each talent that you have been given,
Will you gamble and squander the gift of God
And by selfish ambition be driven?

Or will you choose the higher road
Of sacrifice and humility?
Will you lay down your life and all you own
To receive God's life and tranquility?

You cannot serve both God and mammon;
If you gamble you will lose.
And if you love most the things of this world,
Then the things of this world you will choose.

But if you have tasted God's goodness
And have drunk of the waters of life,
And you know that Christ is the fountain
That frees us from all sin and strife.

And if you know God's Word is true,
If you'll trust in His love, He will take you
Into His own glorious Promised Land.
He will never leave nor forsake you.

With God there is no gamble;
His every word is true.
And I will dare to trust my life
Into His hands—will you?

> Trust in the LORD with all thine heart; and lean not unto thine own understanding. In all thy ways acknowledge him, and he shall direct thy paths. (Proverbs 3:5–6)
>
> No man can serve two masters: for either he will hate the one, and love the other; or else he will hold to the one, and despise the other. Ye cannot serve God and mammon. Therefore I say unto you, Take no thought for your life, what ye shall eat, or what ye shall drink; nor yet for your body, what ye shall put on. Is not the life more than meat, and the body than raiment? Behold the fowls of the air: for they sow not, neither do they reap, nor gather into barns; yet your heavenly Father feedeth them. Are ye not much better than they? Which of you by taking thought can add one cubit unto his stature? And why take ye thought for raiment? Consider the lilies of the field, how they grow; they toil not, neither do they spin: And yet I say unto you, That even Solomon in all his glory was not arrayed like one of these. Wherefore, if God so clothe the grass of the field, which to day is, and to morrow is cast into the oven, shall he not much more clothe you,

O ye of little faith? Therefore take no thought, saying, What shall we eat? or, What shall we drink? or, Wherewithal shall we be clothed? (For after all these things do the Gentiles seek:) for your heavenly Father knoweth that ye have need of all these things. But seek ye first the kingdom of God, and his righteousness; and all these things shall be added unto you. Take therefore no thought for the morrow: for the morrow shall take thought for the things of itself. Sufficient unto the day is the evil thereof. (Matthew 6:24–34)

WORDS

May the Lord be praised and magnified,
And in my every word be glorified.

Let all that from these lips of flesh proceed
Be truth, which His own divine mouth has decreed.

With uplifting speech, not finding fault,
But graciously flavored and seasoned with salt.

For the words of a fool cause dissension and strife,
But the righteous mouth is a fountain of life.

A fool's way is right in his own eyes,
But he who holds his tongue is wise.

The foolish repeat all the gossip they hear,
Carrying tales and corrupting the ear.

From the fruit of the lips, the wise man is filled
With good things from the earth that his own hands have tilled.

And someday, when the Lord of the harvest appears
To gather the fruit we've produced through the years,

May He find in abundance delightfully sweet
Words that are pure and pleasant to eat.

> A good man out of the good treasure of his heart bringeth forth that which is good; and an evil man out of the evil treasure of his heart bringeth forth

that which is evil: for of the abundance of the heart his mouth speaketh. (Luke 6:45)

By him therefore let us offer the sacrifice of praise to God continually, that is, the fruit of our lips giving thanks to his name. (Hebrews 13:15)

A man shall eat good by the fruit of his mouth: but the soul of the transgressors shall eat violence. (Proverbs 13:2)

Wounded Pride

There is a vanity I find
Insidiously persistent,
To which most of us are blind
And few of us resistant.

Concerning that which we prefer
To overlook and hide;
Yet when offended, we refer
To the offender's pride.

The innocence that we proclaim
On our part is, in fact,
A subtle way to place the blame
So as to counteract.

I see no way the Lord has made
For injured pride to win;
Though with sweetness overlaid,
The Lord still calls it sin.

> The discretion of a man deferreth his anger; and [it is] his glory to pass over a transgression. (Proverbs 19:11)

> A brother offended [is harder to be won] than a strong city: and [their] contentions [are] like the bars of a castle. (Proverbs 18:19)

> Also take no heed unto all words that are spoken; lest thou hear thy servant curse thee. (Ecclesiastes 7:21–22)

> Moreover if thy brother shall trespass against thee, go and tell him his fault between thee and him alone: if he shall hear thee, thou hast gained thy brother. (Matthew 18:15–17)

> For where envying and strife [is], there [is] confusion and every evil work. (James 3:16)

> Thou shalt not avenge, nor bear any grudge against the children of thy people, but thou shalt love thy neighbour as thyself: I [am] the LORD. (Leviticus 19:18)

About the Author

Bet Howard Amante is a 1957 graduate of Bay City High School and attended John Robert Powers Modeling School in Dallas, Texas, where she also worked as a flight attendant for Texas International Airlines. She is a native Texan whose background includes an early participation in beauty pageantry.

At the age of sixteen, she was trained and coached by fashion model Addy Miller and won her first big pageant as Miss Galveston Splash Day. As a result, Bet became a successful model and enjoyed a career in fashion, photography, and television. Bet has also enjoyed a later career in marketing and interior design.

She is married to Gene Amante, retired executive of a major chemical company and jazz musician, with whom she shares a delightfully diversified family of eight children, ten grandchildren, and one white standard poodle, "Diva," Le Divinité Dulce Bella.

Bet has been a serious student of the scriptures for forty-two years. Her love of writing stems from her love of God and people and the encouragement of her dear friend and mentor, actress Jeanette Clift George, founder of the AD Players at Grace Theatre in Houston, Texas.

Personal experience as a Bible teacher and speaker to both adults and children initiated a desire to articulately express the power of love, the rewards of virtue, and the benefits of believing.

An ordained minister, author of inspirational poetry, originator and coordinator of the Glory Chain Prayer Ministry, past leader of the Servants' Heart Women's Ministry of Faith West Church, Bet served four years as vice president and program chairman of Weston Lakes Christian Women's Outreach, Inc., as well as elder and deacon of restoration under Pastor Carolyn Sissom at the historical Little White Church (Eastgate Ministries) on LH7 Ranch in Barker, Texas, for ten years.

Bet is a collector of antiques, loves art, is an avid gardener, and loves to cook and entertain friends and visitors in her home in West Houston. At seventy-five, she remains actively involved in her family life and her community, and continues to serve the body of believers in the Lord Jesus Christ, and as elder and deacon in Eastgate Ministries.

Blessed be the name of the Lord my God
Who has brought me out of darkness into light
Blessed be the name of the Lord my God
who has taught my hands to war and my fingers to fight

I love You my wonderful Lord

Printed in the United States
By Bookmasters